THE GERSHWIN COLLECTION

15 EMBRACEABLE CLASSICS ARRANGED BY PHILLIP KEVEREN

— PIANO LEVEL —
LATE INTERMEDIATE/EARLY ADVANCED

Cover photo: Photofest, Inc.

ISBN 978-1-4950-1726-1

Visit Hal Leonard Online at
www.halleonard.com

Visit Phillip at
www.phillipkeveren.com

Contact us:
Hal Leonard
7777 West Bluemound Road
Milwaukee, WI 53213
Email: info@halleonard.com

In Europe, contact:
Hal Leonard Europe Limited
42 Wigmore Street
Marylebone, London, W1U 2RN
Email: info@halleonardeurope.com

In Australia, contact:
Hal Leonard Australia Pty. Ltd.
4 Lentara Court
Cheltenham, Victoria, 3192 Australia
Email: info@halleonard.com.au

PREFACE

George and Ira Gershwin helped define the musical template of the Jazz Age. From 1924 until George's death in 1937, the brothers crafted over two dozen scores for Broadway and Hollywood. The songs that emerged from this period became the backbone of the Great American Songbook.

In the process of writing these arrangements, I became an even bigger Gershwin fan than I was at the outset of the project. These songs were built to last!

Great songs. A piano. Together – magic. Who could ask for anything more?

Sincerely,

Phillip Keveren

BIOGRAPHY

Phillip Keveren, a multi-talented keyboard artist and composer, has composed original works in a variety of genres from piano solo to symphonic orchestra. Mr. Keveren gives frequent concerts and workshops for teachers and their students in the United States, Canada, Europe, and Asia. Mr. Keveren holds a B.M. in composition from California State University Northridge and a M.M. in composition from the University of Southern California.

CONTENTS

BUT NOT FOR ME

from GIRL CRAZY

Music and Lyrics by GEORGE GERSHWIN
and IRA GERSHWIN
Arranged by Phillip Keveren

Freely (♩ = c. 112)

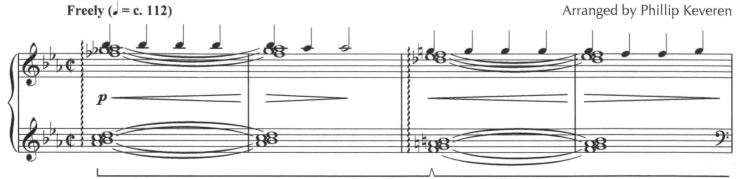

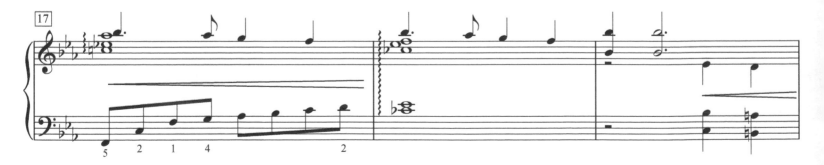

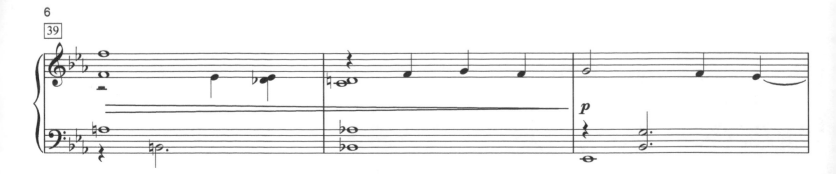

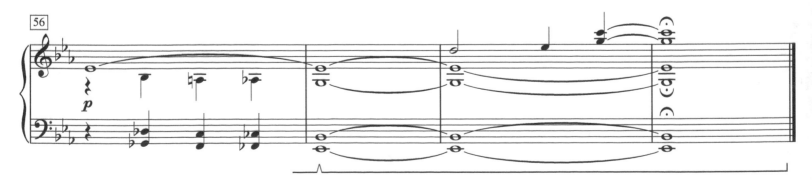

BY STRAUSS
from THE SHOW IS ON

Music and Lyrics by GEORGE GERSHWIN
and IRA GERSHWIN
Arranged by Phillip Keveren

Viennese Waltz (♩ = c. 152-160)

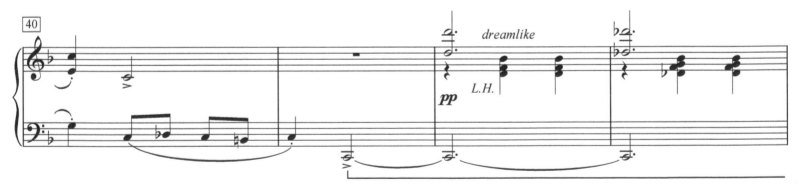

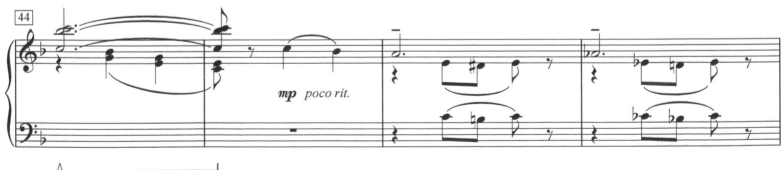

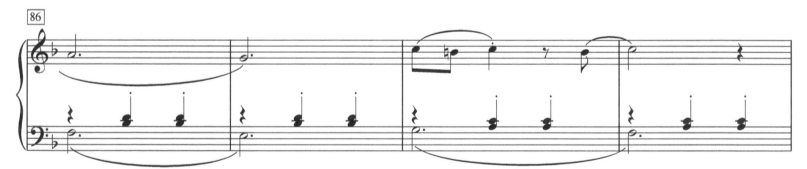

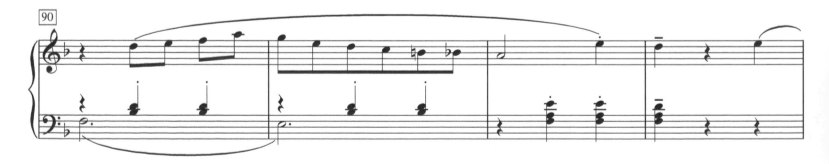

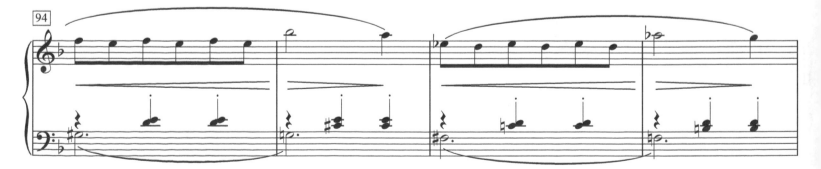

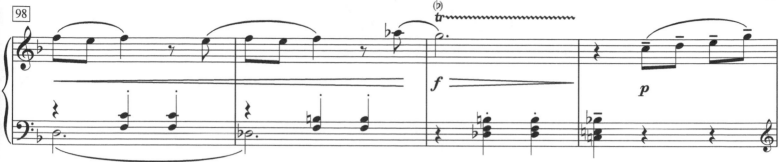

EMBRACEABLE YOU
from CRAZY FOR YOU

Music and Lyrics by GEORGE GERSHWIN
and IRA GERSHWIN
Arranged by Phillip Keveren

Tenderly (♩ = c. 112)

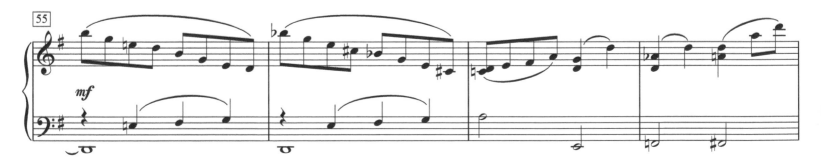

FASCINATING RHYTHM
from RHAPSODY IN BLUE

Music and Lyrics by GEORGE GERSHWIN
and IRA GERSHWIN
Arranged by Phillip Keveren

Snappy (♩ = 152)

I GOT RHYTHM
from AN AMERICAN IN PARIS

Music and Lyrics by GEORGE GERSHWIN
and IRA GERSHWIN
Arranged by Phillip Keveren

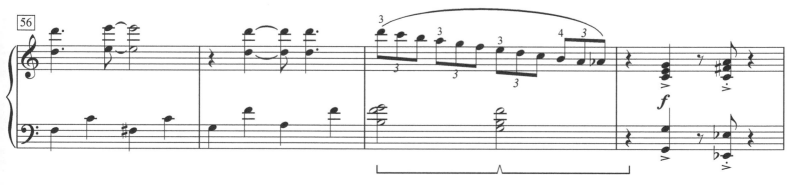

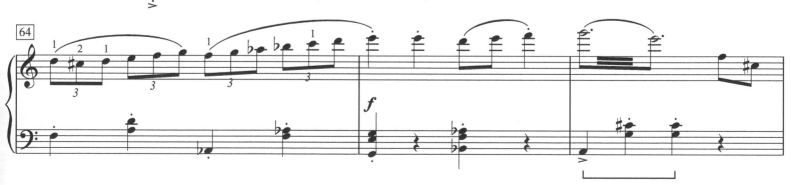

A FOGGY DAY

(In London Town)

from A DAMSEL IN DISTRESS

Music and Lyrics by GEORGE GERSHWIN
and IRA GERSHWIN
Arranged by Phillip Keveren

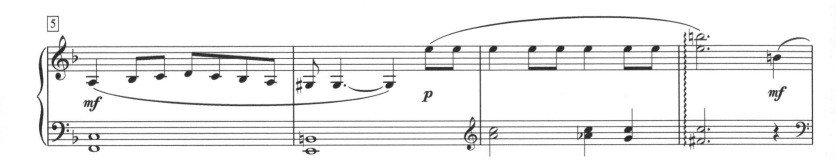

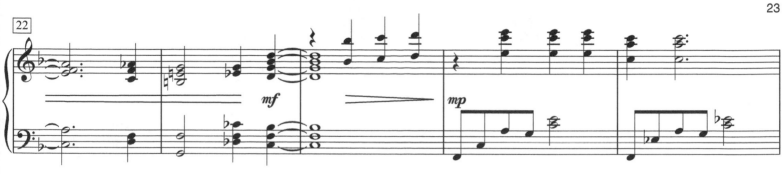

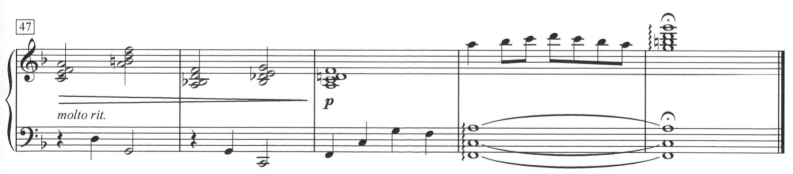

HOW LONG HAS THIS BEEN GOING ON?

from ROSALIE

Music and Lyrics by GEORGE GERSHWIN
and IRA GERSHWIN
Arranged by Phillip Keveren

Jazz ballad (♩ = 72)

I'VE GOT A CRUSH ON YOU

from STRIKE UP THE BAND

Music and Lyrics by GEORGE GERSHWIN
and IRA GERSHWIN
Arranged by Phillip Keveren

LOVE IS HERE TO STAY

from GOLDWYN FOLLIES

Music and Lyrics by GEORGE GERSHWIN
and IRA GERSHWIN
Arranged by Phillip Keveren

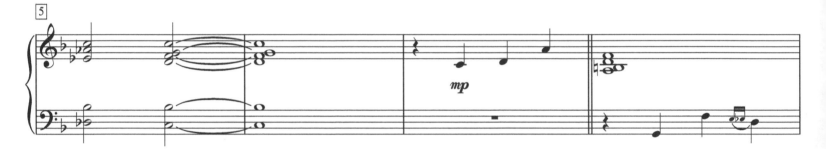

THE MAN I LOVE

from LADY BE GOOD

Music and Lyrics by GEORGE GERSHWIN
and IRA GERSHWIN
Arranged by Phillip Keveren

Freely, expressively (♩ = c. 84)

With pedal

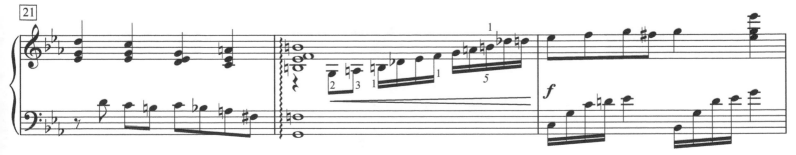

32

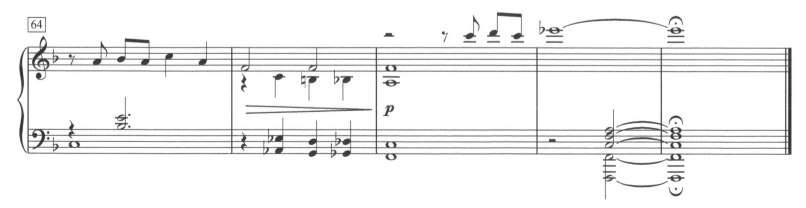

NICE WORK IF YOU CAN GET IT

from A DAMSEL IN DISTRESS

Music and Lyrics by GEORGE GERSHWIN
and IRA GERSHWIN
Arranged by Phillip Keveren

34

'S WONDERFUL
from FUNNY FACE

Music and Lyrics by GEORGE GERSHWIN
and IRA GERSHWIN
Arranged by Phillip Keveren

Passionately, with rubato (♩ = c. 96-104)

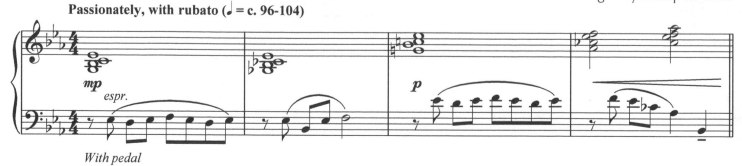

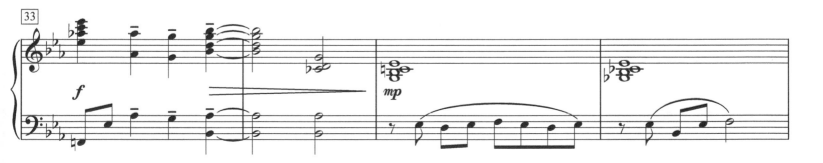

SOMEONE TO WATCH OVER ME
from OH, KAY!

Music and Lyrics by GEORGE GERSHWIN
and IRA GERSHWIN
Arranged by Phillip Keveren

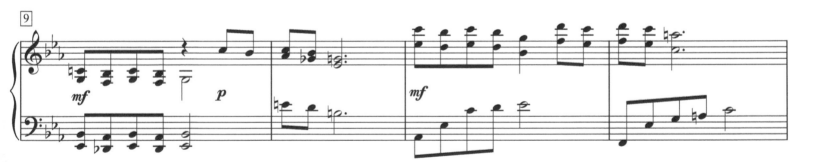

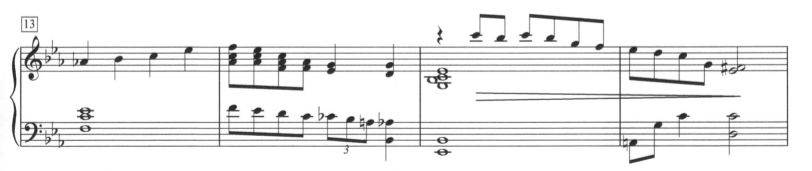

THEY CAN'T TAKE THAT AWAY FROM ME

from THE BARKLEYS OF BROADWAY

Music and Lyrics by GEORGE GERSHWIN
and IRA GERSHWIN
Arranged by Phillip Keveren

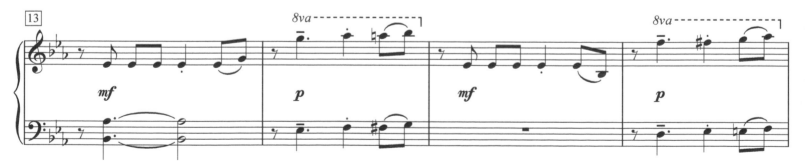

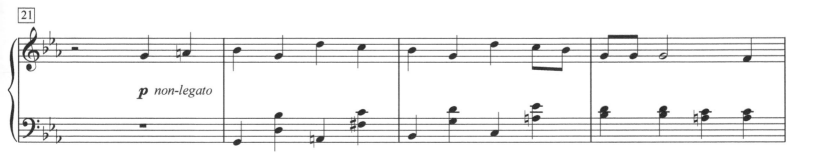

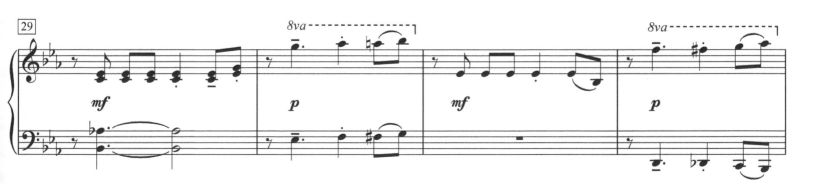

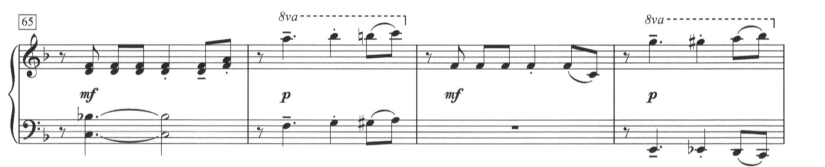

STRIKE UP THE BAND
from STRIKE UP THE BAND

Music and Lyrics by GEORGE GERSHWIN
and IRA GERSHWIN
Arranged by Phillip Keveren

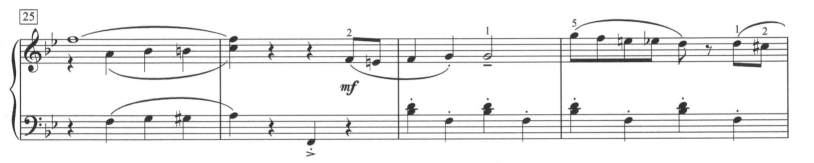

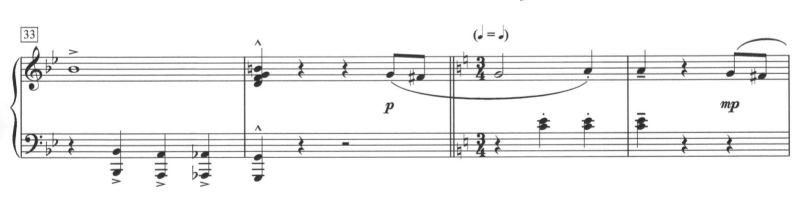

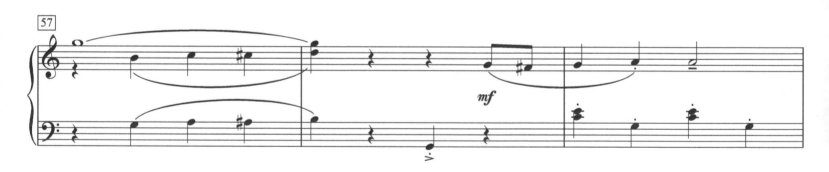